BEVERLY HILLS

BEVERLY HILLS POSTMATE

My Exploration of Beverly Hills and Vicinity Using
Food Delivery Apps

CHARLES ST. ANTHONY

Edited by Marcella Hammer

ISBN 9798710387788

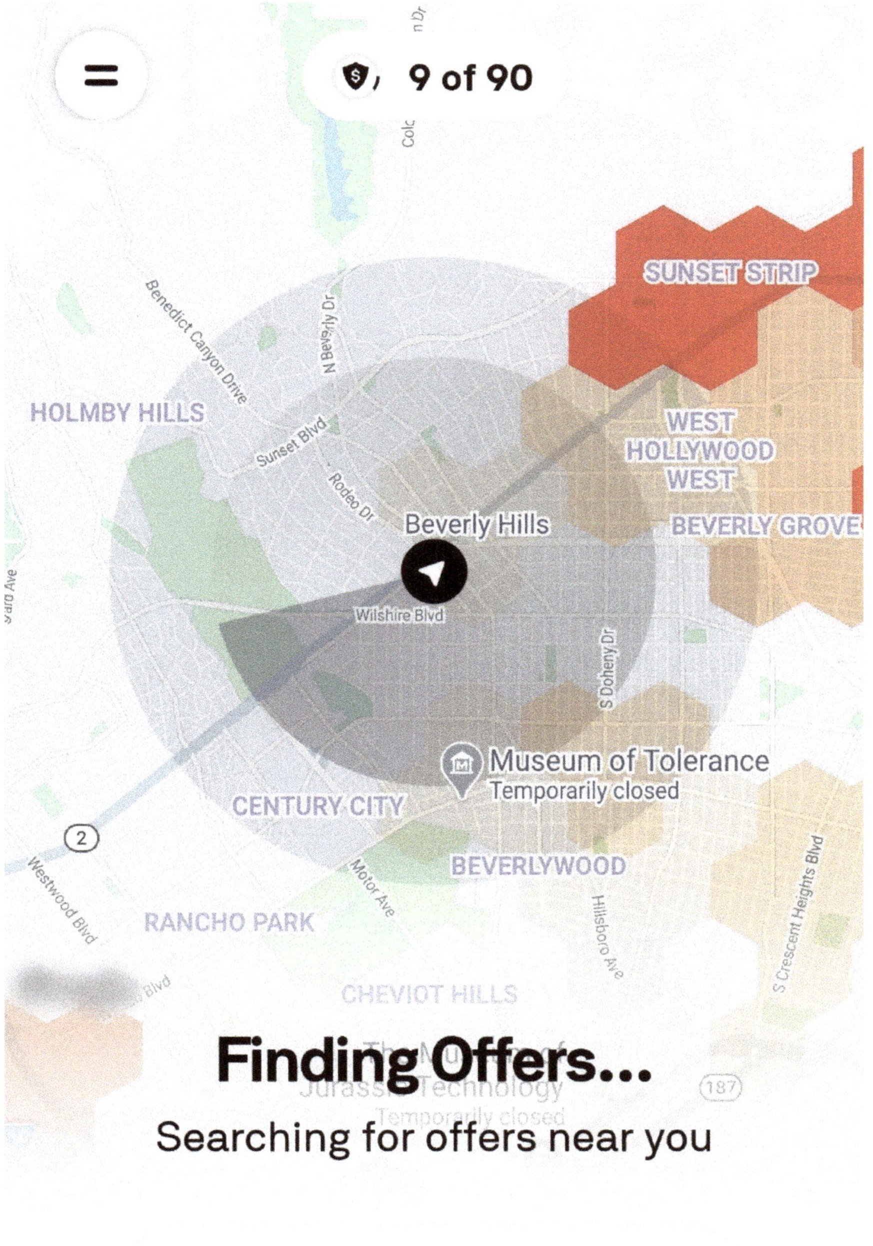
9 of 90
SUNSET STRIP
HOLMBY HILLS
WEST HOLLYWOOD WEST
BEVERLY GROVE
Beverly Hills
Museum of Tolerance
Temporarily closed
CENTURY CITY
BEVERLYWOOD
RANCHO PARK
CHEVIOT HILLS
Finding Offers...
Searching for offers near you
Go Offline

TABLE OF CONTENTS

Instafart

I cracked.

After a couple years of being absolutely determined to get around Los Angeles solely via mass transit, coronavirus made me break down and buy a car. News of COVID-19 made me view the transit system as viral incubation chambers. This got me back into driving. Also, one too many incidents of meth-crazed homeless people shouting at me on the LA Metro pushed me over the edge.

I believe that Los Angeles will have a stellar mass transit system by 2030. Once the purple D Train (we love riding purple D) whisks riders from downtown through Beverly Hills and over to Westwood in twenty-five minutes. Once the Crenshaw Line connects LAX to the rest of the region. And once a method of transit from the San Fernando Valley allows people to bypass the 405 corridor comes to fruition. Then America's second most populous city will have a transit system that makes it worthwhile for most residents to ride. But the present year was 2020 not 2030, and LA's Metro was still wildly impractical for many residents. This, coupled with a deadly virus that had brought activity to a grinding halt, led me to take advantage of a local dealer's financing on an electric vehicle. I bought a Chevy Bolt in a flashy color they marketed as "kinetic blue."

I hadn't driven since a car accident in 2017, when a drunk driver T-boned my car in San Jose rendering it a total loss. Strangely, getting used to driving again in 2020 was relatively easy, as fewer cars inhabited the locked-down streets of LA. However, I had not particularly intended to drive a car again, since I am an environmentalist and wanted to live a car-free lifestyle. The only way I would drive again was with an electric vehicle which I could charge for free at ports my day job kindly provided. Ecstatic as I was not to be contributing to smog and climate change, I felt at every turn someone was reaching into my pocket in this new car purchase. I paid the monthly car note, of course. Car insurance cost nearly double what I paid in San Jose, plus an additional $50 per month to insure myself for app-based gig work. If I wanted the benefits of theft protection, I needed to spring another $30 for OnStar's service which also provided the car's Wi-Fi. And damn it, it feels as if terrestrial radio has a death wish with the absurdly irritating commercials they play on FM. I'll always have a soft spot for Los Angeles' venerable alt-rock station KROQ, but you're almost forced to spring for Sirius XM or Spotify. The commercials on regular radio annoy you into submission.

All these expenses meant that I had to shoehorn an additional $800 into my budget per month, when money was already tight and some of my regular income streams were on hold due to the pandemic. I had supplemented my income by performing as an extra on TV, and with all of Hollywood indefinitely on hiatus that entire income had dried up completely. A new income stream had to be found *tout de suite*!

First I tried delivering for Instacart, or as I call it Instafart—I know, real mature. I signed up to work as an Instacart shopper, and after the obligatory background check, Instacart anointed me with a grasshopper green Instacart credit card. When you shop for customers, you use the fake credit card to pay at the register then send a photo of the receipt to the company. Along with the credit card came a green Instacart lanyard with a carrot on it that went promptly in the garbage bin. If there is one way not to get laid in Los Angeles, it is to walk around with a green Instacart lanyard swinging from your neck.

Instacart almost made me have a mental breakdown, because I found the Los Angeles market had too many "points of failure"— designated places where you can mess up and they deactivate you. This is when I learned how out of sync the stock of most supermarkets is with the Instacart shopping experience. Mainly due to grocery shortages, about one-third of items on the customers' orders would not be available once I arrived at the supermarket. It wasn't just orders for things such as toilet paper and disinfecting wipes that would be out. Everyday items like garlic would be out. Any time people asked for something "organic," it usually wasn't there. Delivering regular iceberg lettuce when someone asked for "organic iceberg lettuce" is a great way to get a complaint on Instacart in LA. We take that organic shit seriously.

Instacart shoppers can communicate with customers on their phones while shopping to avoid organic iceberg lettuce mishaps, but unfortunately, customers aren't necessarily glued to their phones during your shopping trips. Many times they will miss your message as to whether they want a replacement or whether they want you to cancel that item in their order. This leads to many executive decisions on the part of an Instacart shopper.

I had to make several such hard decisions on one trip to CVS Pharmacy for a customer we'll call "Karen" (not her real name). Karen had asked for a kid's toothpaste with *Paw Patrol* cartoon dog characters on it. Seeing that CVS had sold out *Paw Patrol* toothpaste, I messaged Karen through the app and asked if she wanted *Sesame Street* toothpaste instead. No reply. Some of the chocolate she requested was out, so I didn't pick up as many bon bons as Karen wanted. Of course, after the delivery she complained about the *Sesame Street* toothpaste and implied I was stealing chocolate (she never paid for the chocolate she didn't receive). Instacart Karen messed with my shopper rating.

What truly had me saying fuck Instacart was the fact that having the app on and plugging my phone into my car via USB *would cause my phone to overheat and shut down* in the middle of my orders. Having your phone out of commission while you are trying to follow Google Maps to drive somewhere is not a delight. Now I can't say whether it's the fault of the app, my car, or my phone, but at any rate my Instafart experience was extremely *no bueno*, so I put my career as an Instacart shopper on ice after about thirty deliveries.

I didn't want to die from a deadly virus, so I didn't want to give up my kinetic blue Chevy Bolt. But how was I going to come up with an extra $800 per month while the economy was in the shit can. Then I had a eureka moment! What if I get my electric car to pay for itself by delivering Postmates in America's most exclusive zip code: 90210! I could be raking in the tips while learning about the *crème de la crème* of Los Angeles food culture at the same time.

The gauntlet had been thrown. I would Postmate in Beverly Hills.

So Who's Beverly?

Everybody knows there is a city in Southern California called Beverly Hills. But what do you *ACTUALLY* know about it? Possibly you know its zip code 90210. You might know some hillbillies occupied the region. Images of movies such as *Pretty Woman* and *Beverly Hills Cop* come to mind. But do you really know anything more about it than the fact that it is an expensive place to live, with some designer clothing shops? Is Beverly Hills a place that you have heard about your whole life, but when pressed you don't really know anything specific about it? That was the case for me when embarking on this project, so let's look at the lay of the land, shall we?

First of all, Beverly Hills is small. The population hovers around 34,000—if Beverly Hills were a country it would be slightly more populous than San Marino (28,000) and slightly less populous than Liechtenstein (35,000). Beverly Hills takes up just 5.7 square miles (14.8 square kilometers)—that makes it slightly larger than London Heathrow Airport (4.7 square miles) and slightly smaller than the Pacific Island nation of Nauru (6 square miles).

Beverly Hills being so physically small presented a challenge in doing research. Full-disclosure: the deliveries in this study were not entirely inside Beverly Hills itself. If a Beverly Hills-based restaurant pinged me, the drop off might be anywhere within a twenty mile radius.

If I were dropping off at a house or apartment in Beverly Hills, the ping might come from the city of West Hollywood, or from the nearby neighborhoods in Los Angeles such as Westwood. So it might be best to think of Beverly Hills as the epicenter of my case study, with the restaurants and customers I interacted with spiralling outwards from there.

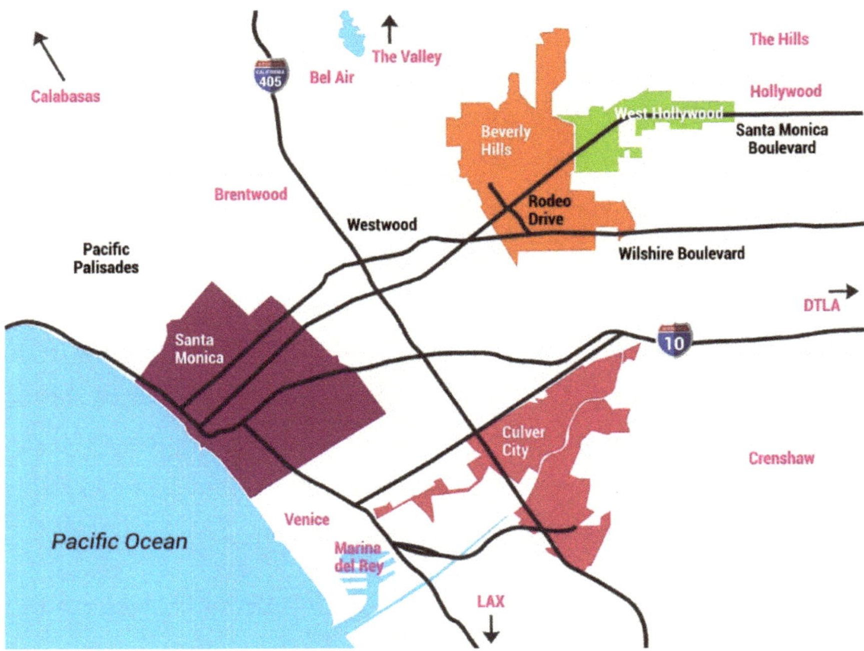

To conduct this exploration of food culture, I would position my car somewhere in the boundaries of Beverly Hills and turn on the apps I drive for: Uber Eats, DoorDash, and Postmates. Delivery drivers call this "multi-apping"—whoever pinged me first was the winner, and I would go pick up from the restaurant and speed over to drop it off at the customer's house.

Looking at the map of Beverly Hills one might be inclined to ask, "For why is this city completely surrounded by Los Angeles?" The city of Los Angeles borders Beverly Hills on all sides, except the east side where the city of West Hollywood perches. The TLDR answer is water. As depicted in Jack Nicholson's classic, *Chinatown*, much of Los Angeles' early politics revolved around providing water to the rapidly increasing population of the arid region the city now sits.

The long answer is much more intriguing. Clasp my hand dear reader, as I guide you down the rabbit hole of Beverly History. Trust me, it's a nice hole.

After the Spanish began settling in what was a region inhabited by the Tongva tribe, an Afro Latina widow named Maria Rita Valdez Villa received the deed for the Beverly Hills area then known as "Rodeo de las Aguas" or "Gathering of the Waters." The area actually had its own underground streams—all the better for Maria Rita's cowboys and livestock to roam about in. Things were all good and dandy until Native Americans launched an assault on the rancho, and Maria Rita was all "Fuck this!" and dipped.

She sold the land to Benjamin D. Wilson and Henry Hancock for $4,000, two gentlemen who became the namesakes for Mt. Wilson and Hancock Park. An online inflation calculator informs me $4,000 would fetch about $124,000 in today's money. Nothing to sneeze at, but still not enough to buy even a single house in today's Beverly Hills where the average home fetches $4,800,000. So Maria Rita could get like 1/50th of a home in today's market for what she sold the land that became the entire city for in 1854. Today that money would get maybe a closet.

Years passed and various developers and ranching types tried to develop the land, but it was still kind of a hard sell. Situated a good twelve miles west of DTLA's early settlements, the area that is now Beverly Hills was still mostly coyotes and tumbleweeds. There was even a period when some developers tried to name it "Morocco Junction," but the old rancho mostly sat undeveloped. Around 1900, a developer and his wife named it "Beverly Hills" after the lovely area called Beverly Farms in Massachusetts. This place in Massachusetts, in turn, was named after the village of Beverley in Yorkshire, UK. In Ye Olde English, the town in Yorkshire was named after "Bevreli" or "Beverlac" which meant "Beaver Clearing" or "Beaver Lake." So there you have it. Beverly Hills is all about beaver.

Back in 1900, Beverly Hills was still total dullsville until they built the Beverly Hills Hotel in 1912. The city incorporated in 1914, and a racetrack opened, drawing crowds to the area. Early film stars Douglas Fairbanks and Mary Pickford staked their claim at an estate called Pickfair, which gave rise to a deluge of movie stars from the silent era into the area, including Charlie Chaplain, Gloria Swanson, and Rudolph Valentino.

Terror struck early Beverly Hills, when *gasp* the city of Los Angeles almost annexed the fledgling township in 1923. "Look at all this water we have," LA said, "Just come be part of Los Angeles. It won't hurt. We promise." Hollywood and Venice were once their own towns, and Los Angeles annexed them. Would the same fate befall Beverly Hills?

Mary Pickford and Douglas Fairbanks would have NONE OF THIS, since having their own town made it easier to control information that got out about them. Even though they eventually got married, Pickford and Fairbanks originally shacked up while having an adulterous affair which raised eyebrows. Movie studios would not stand for "America's Sweetheart" actually being known as a wanton jezebel that showed her ankles like a trollop and slept with married men. The two were keen to avoid any negative publicity, so having a small town away from LA's city center where they could control things and cavort in peace was one motive for keeping the town separate.

Anyway, Mary and Douglas were all, "We've got our own water, and we don't want LA to swallow us amoeba-like into their fold." They led a crusade against annexing into Los Angeles with their famous friends and Mary and Doug's mega-watt star power won out. Thanks to the efforts of Mary Pickford and Douglas Fairbanks, Beverly Hills still exists in all its glory smack in the middle of Los Angeles as uniquely its own entity.

So the long answer as to why Beverly Hills exists as it does: moist waters, British beaver, and tawdry adultery. *Plus ça change, plus c'est la même chose.*

Beverly Hills on a Budget

Now we come to the most delicious portion of my book! Where I introduce meals I discovered while doing deliveries. Considering the nation is going through an economic crisis, I thought best not to introduce extremely expensive items here. Not that I wouldn't love to try *Wagyu* ribeye drizzled in truffled cream sauce in the name of research, I thought introducing meals that cost several hundred dollars would not be welcomed with open arms by the public in the current economic climate. So today I bring you a more egalitarian menu that anyone could afford if splurging on a nice lunch, so all these offerings are under $30. *Voilà, mes chéries*, it is time for you to experience "Beverly Hills on a Budget!"

Red Velvet Cupcake

Sprinkles Cupcakes

9635 Santa Monica Blvd. Beverly Hills, CA

Ingredients: Southern style light chocolate cake with cream cheese frosting.

Plant-based alternative: Vegan red velvet.

Purple and Blue Salad

Wally's Beverly Hills

447 North Canon Drive, Beverly Hills

Ingredients: Roasted beets, blueberries, grapes, red cabbage, pickled cucumber, buffalo milk blue cheese, pistachio, aged balsamic, and olive oil.

Lemon Chicken Plate

California Pita

242 South Beverly Drive, Beverly Hills

Ingredients: marinated chicken breast, warm pita, special sauce, salad, and choice of white or brown rice.

Plant-based alternative: Falafel plate.

An's Famous Garlic Noodles™

Crustacean

468 North Bedford Drive, Beverly Hills

Ingredients: Roasted Garlic, An's Secret Sauce (vegetarian-friendly).

An's Famous Garlic Noodles™ wins the Beverly Hills Postmate's most highly recommended menu item, since these noodles had me thinking about them several days later. They have a subtle tang that is difficult to describe but completely delicious. The noodles on

Crustacean's "An the Go" takeout menu are $22. I am a hearty eater, so they wouldn't make a whole meal for me, but they make a splendid side dish.

For a full lunch at a reasonable price try California Pita. I discovered the Lemon Chicken plate at California Pita's Brentwood location, and since then I have been arguing it is the best lunch on the Westside of Los Angeles, for its value. California Pita operates locations in Beverly Hills, Brentwood, DTLA, and Woodland Hills.

If you want to feel like you're truly in Beverly Hills, you have a wonderful view of street activity from a table at Wally's. Wally's Purple and Blue Salad is large enough for a couple people to split, and Wally's takeaway and delivery orders come with the bonus of a little package of seasoned popcorn.

The commercial district centered around Rodeo Drive has the big names fashionista's adore such as Chanel, Dior, Vuitton, and Gucci. You don't necessarily need to spend that kind of money to feel like a Material Girl—just use Sprinkles Cupcakes' ATM to order sweets. It's a socially distant way to get your hands on their coveted red velvet and dark chocolate cupcakes for around $5 a pop.

Some of my favorite food discoveries in my research came from outside the borders of Beverly Hills, as well. Burger joints were the most popular type of food in my study, and Mexican food was number two. Mexican represented 14% of my orders. The Mexican establishment with the most devoted fan base was a food truck operating near Brentwood called El Paladar Oaxaqueño which translates to "The Palate of Oaxaca State." I went to El Paladar five times, but each time I went there I would end up dropping off the food in a different corner of the city. I personally vouch for their tacos *al pastor* if you enjoy meat, and if you swing vegan, their plant-based wet burrito comes with a vermilion-colored sauce with a nice punch.

Chocolate Bash was the most popular dessert stop in this study, and its shop on Pico Boulevard in western Los Angeles buzzes with orders of crêpes, shakes, and chocolate-covered strawberries.

Other food discoveries include vegetarian burgers at Honeybee Burger which can be picked up at 11419 Santa Monica in West Los Angeles, it's currently my favorite burger in LA. They also serve "Frots" which are an ingenious mix of French fries and tater tots. Let's just all bow down right now. Even though it is called Honeybee Burger, no bees were harmed in the making of this burger. Their website notes all the food is 100% plant-based. Honeybee Burger usurped the crown of best burger from Window (the restaurant's name is stylized as Win ~ dow) on Rose Avenue in Venice. You will have a "Los Angeles" moment when you see you can swap French fries for a kale salad (I actually quite like the kale salad). In this case being #2 is still a winner, as typing about Window's double cheeseburger is making me hungry as we speak.

The "Close but No Cigar" award goes to Fat Sal's Deli in Westwood. I had been eager to try this establishment, since every time I picked up a delivery from them a large line of UCLA students snaked along the sidewalk. I tried the "Fat Jaime"—a sandwich featuring thinly-sliced steak, grilled onions, a bit of bacon, and even an egg. The experience was extremely tasty, but a little too rich for my stomach, so, Fat Jaime just barely missed the top selections of the Beverly Hills Postmate. I'd chow down on Fat Jaime again sometime, though.

Trend Alert!

In contrast to my case study of downtown LA by doing Postmates in 2018 (which you can read in my last humorous short read *DTLA Hustler*), the food courier app business in Los Angeles now feels more mature. During *DTLA Hustler*, it still felt like many of the customers were trendy, young, early-adopter types. Now everyone and their grandma has downloaded Postmates, and Grandma won't stop pestering you to sign up for Drizly with her discount code so she can score a free box of wine. Food courier apps were not a new thing anymore—not only that, the coronavirus lockdown and pandemic made them skyrocket in popularity. Accordingly, the revenue of food delivery apps has soared. MarketWatch describes the trend:

> "DoorDash Inc.'s recent filing for an initial public offering and earnings reports from Uber Technologies Inc., Grubhub Inc., and Postmates have provided a deeper look into delivery apps' business in 2020, and it is clear the pandemic has given the industry a boost. The four companies raked in roughly $5.5 billion in combined revenue from April through September, more than twice as much as their combined $2.5 billion in revenue during the same period last year."

For me as a driver, that means delivering for the courier services was sort of like when you see a documentary about the grizzly bears in Alaska. The documentaries necessarily show the grizzlies wade into the river during salmon mating season, and the bears effortlessly pull out salmon after salmon with great aplomb. This is what it was like doing food deliveries during the pandemic.

Most restaurants I picked up from featured delivery from several apps I dubbed "The Squad of Four": DoorDash, Grubhub, Postmates, and Uber Eats. Postmates constantly pinged me like a festive night of playing *Ms. Pac-Man* at an old school quarter arcade. Tip included, Postmates averaged $6.94 per delivery versus Uber Eats and DoorDash which averaged $7.35 and $6.59, respectively. In the end, Uber Eats was my go-to, because it was almost as busy as Postmates and Uber's average payout per delivery was the highest. Grubhub we shall never know, because there was such a long waiting list of people wanting to be drivers, that I never got to try driving for their app—which is all for the best because Postmates, DoorDash, and Uber Eats kept my kinetic blue Chevy Bolt zipping across Los Angeles throughout 2020.

It's hard to make generalizations about the users of each app, but in my own experience Postmates users tended to be younger, skew female, and slightly more twee. DoorDash was hard to get a read on, but I would say they were more hipster. Uber Eats tended to have more men and looked more professional. There were contradictions to this every night I drove, so if you're an elderly man who loves ordering Postmates, don't @ me. I'm just trying to summarize the experience.

The very survival of some restaurants depended on the food-delivery apps, and it was a common sight to see a small platoon of iPads from each of the delivery apps standing guard on the counters of each restaurant. As orders came in the tablets would produce a name and order, and in turn the platforms queued drivers like myself to come get the food.

In the course of making 506 deliveries for my research data, I noticed some interesting and surprising trends.

1. People in Beverly Hills and the rest of the Westside eat lots of fast food garbage. Before doing this research, I had expected to only be delivering stereotypical food we see the upper crust eat in movies and TV. I had envisioned trips to pick up beluga caviar, Maine Lobster, and Kobe beef. Maybe some *foie gras* only snatched from geese curated by Alpine monks. I know that fast food chains are over-represented in my study, because during the pandemic people were eating a lot of comfort food. I did include deliveries during the dinner rush, and I also had a lot of late night orders from 10PM until 2AM. Let's just say hardly anyone orders anything sensible after 10PM.

   Also, I had a policy of inclusion for my research, so I tried to accept every order that pinged me. Many veteran drivers know better than to accept all orders, and they cherry pick the best offers since you get an estimate for the delivery before you accept. Hence, a lot of shitty Jack in the Box and Taco Bell orders other drivers were skipping came to me. Well, suffice to say people in Beverly Hills and surrounding affluent areas eat just as much greasy shit as the rest of the country. The McDonald's near Century City was the establishment with the most orders. I got the impression that in some cases, the wealthy people just handed their kids a phone when their children balked at eating whatever tempeh and rabbit feed vegan creation the adults might have had their cooks make.

2. Ghost kitchens are a thing. Along Santa Monica Boulevard near the 405 entrance, there's a place called Order Colony where drivers pick up for a large number of restaurants. Multiple restaurants consolidate their pick up at one window. At the time of writing I counted 89 restaurants the website for Order Colony shows available to pick up. Order Colony features some well-known places such as Trejos Tacos and Shin-Sen-Gumi (Ramen), and some that you've never heard of. I picked up from four ghost kitchen style places throughout LA, and they seem to be increasing in popularity, since it makes the prepping-cooking-delivering process that much more seamless.

3. Restaurants now utilize SEO baiting. If you don't know what SEO is, let me put on my nerd glasses for a second. SEO (or Search Engine Optimization) is how you get Google, Yahoo, and other search engines to find your website. There are many methods to improve your SEO, and planting certain keywords in the text is one of the best ways to increase your website's visibility to search engines.

   Delivery-apps now employ something similar to SEO, since restaurants use keywords to match what users search for in the delivery app. The list of Order Colony restaurants includes a lot of generic sounding places such as "LA Pasta." In some cases, these "restaurants" lack an actual physical brick-and-mortar establishment—people ordering on Postmates aren't necessarily searching for a particular restaurant. They are searching for "Wings" or "Vegan Pizza" and just ordering from whatever pops up with nice pictures. And not just ghost kitchens like Order Colony are doing this, your traditional mom-and-pop restaurants are realizing that people don't necessarily search for "Davie's Greek Restaurant"—they will search for "gyro" and order from the closest and most economical place that Postmates displays. I would sometimes go to a restaurant with a name like "Davie's Greek Restaurant," but in fact the customer thinks they are ordering from a place called "Gyro King" (I made up these two names for example's sake). Davie's Greek Restaurant and Gyro King would be one and the same. It was confusing, but one way or another, I got people their gyros.

One time I picked up ice cream from a place that said its name was something like "Froyo Parlor," but there was no actual frozen yogurt spot. It was a freezer in a liquor store with just some Ben & Jerry's and Häagen Dazs in it.

4. Funny names also appear to be *en vogue*. Establishments have capitalized on the SEO baiting by also making the names humorous. I'm all for making up funny names, but I will say I was legit surprised when these pseudo-restaurants started dropping F Bombs. My deliveries included places named "Best F*ckin Pizza" and "F*CK GLUTEN." Another amusing name I came across was "Bitch Don't Grill My Cheese," which is a bit hypocritical for a grilled cheese establishment. Isn't grilling cheese the point? I get it's riffing off the Kendrick Lamar song "Bitch, Don't Kill My Vibe," but this contradiction amused me. Other funny names included Fun Ol' Cakes, El Munchies, Mother Clucker, No Cluck Vegan Chicken, Pimp My Pasta, and Throw Some Cheese on That Bitch.

5. Juvenile food choices are trending upward. This is part of the overall pandemic trend toward "comfort food"—foods that remind people of their childhood were extremely popular. If

you are in the business of grilled cheese or chicken fingers, this is your time to shine.

You know what time it is? It's that time I bring you not just one, but three of my fabulous and educational infographics!

Food Orders

In total there were 177 Orders of French fries including crisscut, crinkle cut, seasoned, curly, and Cajun fries.

Top 5 Fast Food Establishments (Total of Deliveries)

McDonald's	Taco Bell	Jack in the Box	Fatburger	Carl's Jr.
61	36	30	14	11

McDonald's

We had 12 orders of the McFlurry®

Orders of McNuggets: 32

Most Popular McNuggets Dip:
Tangy BBQ Dipping Sauce 35

Taco Bell

Orders with Crunchwrap
Supreme 22 vs. Chalupa 21

Hot Sauce 32 vs Fire Sauce 31

9 Cinnabon Delights

Jack in the Box

14 orders of "2 Tacos"

9 orders of curly fries

6 orders of Buttermilk Ranch
Dipping Sauce

Top 5 Colas

Coca-Cola	Sprite	Mountain Dew Baja Blast	Dr. Pepper	Pepsi
39	20	12	9	6

Alcohol

Most popular alcohol was
White Claw which had 6
orders for White Claw in
raspberry, black cherry,
mango and their popular
variety pack.

Chinese

9 orders of orange
chicken in total from
Chinese and Pan-Asian
restaurants

Starbucks

Starbucks' most popular
drink was Blonde Vanilla
Latte

Pizza

19 Pizzas ordered (Pies or
by the Slice)
Pepperoni was on 7 of
them

Types of Establishments

Burger Joint
27%

Mexican
15%

Chicken/Wings
7%

Pizza
5%

Convenience Store
5%

Mediterranean
4%

Desserts
3%

Liquor Store
3%

Chinese
2%

Ice Cream/Cold Desserts
2%

Sandwich
2%

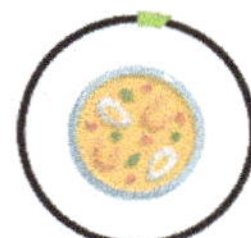

Thai Food
2%

Vietnamese
2%

Other
21%

Payment Breakdown

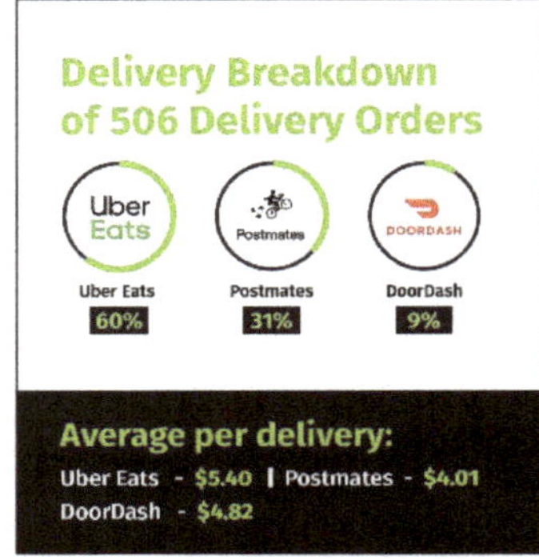

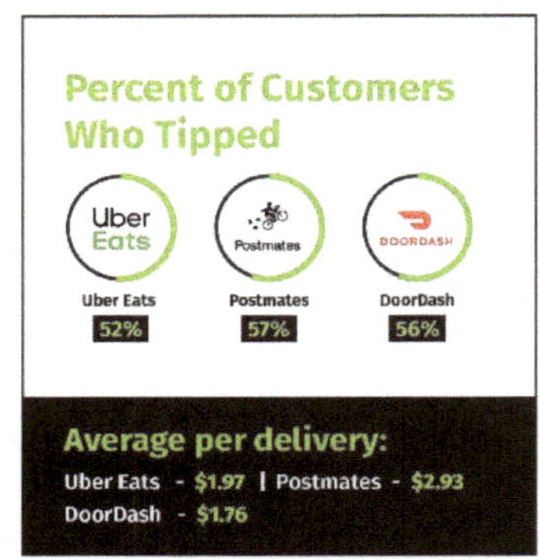

Restaurant whose customer left the best tip:
Avra Beverly Hills Estiatorio: $35.38

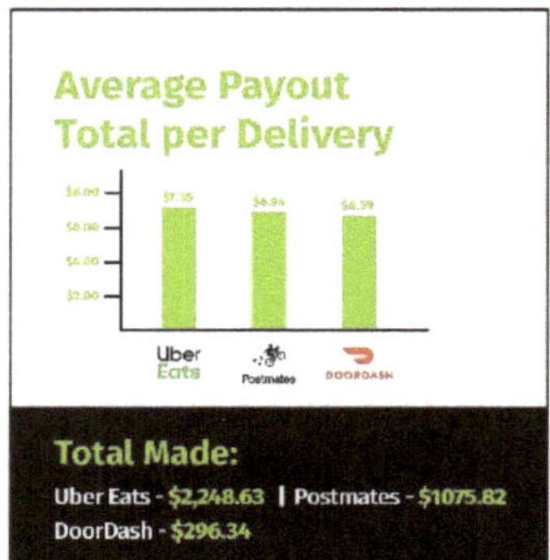

Grand Total Made During Study

$3620.79

Average Distance per Delivery (Uber Eats)
3.5 miles (5.6 km)

Average Duration per Delivery (Uber Eats)
19.5 minutes

Operation Slow as Molasses

Did you know there's a pandemic happening? Just thought I'd bring it up in case you haven't heard. I bet you had no idea— it's pretty underground, I know.

In this chapter, I'm going to present to you some of the struggles of 2020—I worked on *Beverly Hills Postmate* throughout the year, but for some obvious reasons this almost was the book that didn't happen. I'm sure for the rest of our lives, we will think of our life being divided in 2 eras: BR (Before Rona) and AR (After Rona).

I still remember the exact moment I realized the coronavirus was going to be a huge, devastating problem. I had been scanning the news like I normally do, and I remember a story charting the progress of an outbreak in China in January 2020. It showed Wuhan Province in red, followed by results from the next week in which all the provinces surrounding Wuhan were having infections. Then the following week, provinces that ringed all those states had infections. Then the fourth week the coronavirus had infected people in every province in the People's Republic of China. *Holy shit!* I thought *Our country is not ready for this AT ALL.*

That day I went to several pharmacies in downtown Los Angeles, and people had bought all the face masks already. I then checked Amazon, and sellers had jacked up the price of masks to 80 or 100 dollars. I settled on a set of 4 black cotton masks that I ordered from Amazon on January 31, 2020 for $52.99. On March 11, California suffered its first death from COVID-19, and on March 20th Mayor Eric Garcetti issued the "Safer at Home" order. I bought my electric vehicle the first week of April. This was all back when President #45 kept assuring us that the pandemic would be over by Easter.

You might be asking why I would brave the wilds of Los Angeles doing Instacart, Postmates, and Uber Eats when a deadly virus plagued our nation. In addition to the need for money, eventually I realized at some point that either A. I already had COVID back in January or B. I was one of those asymptomatic types.

I worked with the public on a daily basis, and fortunately, I keep testing negative. Even though my mask game and hand washing skills were on fleek, I worked in a highly infectious environment. Then I remembered back in January, before coronavirus became big news, when I had caught a very severe cold. I can recall the exact moment I became infected.

I chatted to a friend who stood near me, and he said, "I just got over a sinus infection." I stood just a foot away from him—when they have breath diagrams on TV to show how infectious the coronavirus is, I was standing in the middle of where his breath cloud would plume out. Five hours after this conversation, I had a blazing hot fever and was on my bed with the chills. A couple of my closest friends had the same bug the following week. This contagion was notable in the speed with which it infected people, and I remember it being tenacious and lingering through the next week. I didn't get sick again for the entirety of 2020 despite interacting with the public at my day job and making hundreds of deliveries taking me into restaurants and apartment buildings. I'll never know if I had a dance with Miss Rona or if I was merely asymptomatic.

On top of the whole pandemic, did I mention we had riots in 2020? Lots of them. Beverly Hills got hit, with looters pillaging expensive brand stores such as Balenciaga. They boarded up Rodeo Drive, and I could see lonely looking influencers trying to catch a pic along the street. The big night of the first riots, I drove past the gym I frequent and rioters had broken the windows. By this time the rioting had stopped, and groups of LAPD staked out every corner.

Photos I took on May 31, 2020 showed graffiti about Beverly Hills, with phrases like "Fuck the 1%" and "Eat the Rich" spray painted on banks and buildings.

The entire summer of 2020 felt palpably tense throughout Los Angeles, and just when we hoped things were settling down, the Armenians decided it was their turn to hold some protests. Areas of Wilshire Boulevard near where I work were shut down by angry Armenians protesting outside the Consulate of Azerbaijan. I'm not educated enough on their conflict to really comment, and I'm certain the Armenians had every right to be furious. So I'm only going to say one group or another was protesting all summer long, and it added to everyone's stress level.

The riots and the pandemic created a tense environment for much of the year, increasing the stress I felt while doing deliveries for research. Recurring app malfunctions exacerbated my already worn-out state of mind. Each of the apps has their own set of glitches. For example, Postmates sent me to a restaurant whose staff claimed to not have an agreement in place with Postmates, a bar and grill near East LA. This was in September, so some patrons grazed on bar food outdoors in a patio space. The restaurant had already closed when I arrived, and a waitress said to me, "Bb, we don't take Postmates orders." So why was I there? And then Postmates didn't pay me for this order, since it got canceled.

Another common Postmates glitch happens when the app automatically accepts a couple deliveries at once, but the algorithm switches the pickup to another driver while you are driving to the restaurant. When you arrive at the restaurant, your first order has already been taken by another driver so you need to contact the support team to explain this situation. It was due to all these glitches within the Postmates app causing me to do work I didn't get paid for that I eventually prioritized Uber Eats and DoorDash over Postmates.

Uber Eats generally was the most seamless experience for drivers to make deliveries, especially because they don't force you to pay for meals with a fake credit card. Uber Eats does have its share of glitches. A couple times per week I would be sent to restaurants that had already closed for the night—I'm uncertain if this is a problem on Uber's side or if possibly the restaurant staff did not turn the app off on their end correctly. When this happened with Uber, I would call the Uber support and they would cancel the poor customer's order, but each time I got compensated $3 for my time. Hey, Big Spender! I can finally afford that one taquito I've had my eye on at 7-Eleven.

The result of these obstacles along with the chaotic government of President #45, the Orange One who shall not be named, I believe affected everyone's mental well-being. I call the vague malaise "Rona Brain"—people seemed to be operating in a sort of brain fog. Restaurants blocked off the dining sections of their establishments and created a special zone within the normal dining space for pick ups. Sometimes an elderly member of the staff appeared to be doom scrolling through their news feed and just chilling at some table. The drivers (myself included) and staff seemed to be functioning in some sort of mental haze. It could be hard to get their attention, so sometimes I would have to yell out the customer's name and app I'm driving for, like "DoorDash for Rodney!" The restaurant staff and I would then have a half-discernable conversation through our masks where we ended up sounding like the adults in a Charlie Brown cartoon.

I know I suffered from Rona Brain, because I had such a difficult time writing this essay—like I felt almost physical pain in my mind while trying to write. I would have to bribe myself with pizza or açaí bowls to get myself to sit down and write.

I believe the scientific name for the vaccine rollout is a "clusterfuck." Honestly, I was about to fly to St. Petersburg to get my hands on some black market Sputnik vaccine. I know a lot of Westerners might not have trusted a Russian vaccine, but they had something possibly effective out back in July 2020. Russians are intelligent people that always win in chess tournaments and stuff like that, so I feel like we should have given Sputnik more of a chance.

In January 2021, I asked my doctor in a phone appointment about how to get on the waitlist for a vaccine, and Doc said, "You can check the website," which is my personal pet peeve, because that's what the heffa at Wells Fargo says when she doesn't feel like helping you over the phone. I hold a master's degree. *I AM AWARE* there is a website. To set up my appointment I sat on hold for thirty minutes, entered the last four digits of my social five times, gave them my birthday twice, and spelled out my mother's maiden name to some robot. I don't appreciate people who point out there is a website, when I need their help with something. Everyone knows they're just fobbing your problem off onto someone else, but I guess it's more diplomatic than saying, "I can't do shit for you." I was hoping for at least an indication of when this *Groundhog's Day*-like tomfoolery would finally be finished. Doctors like him are the real heroes, and I realize his hands were tied, but it didn't make the situation any less frustrating.

I have to applaud the world-class shade of the vaccine-makers Pfizer and Moderna. They knew that announcing their vaccine results before the presidential election would help the Tangerine Menace, so Pfizer announced their results the week after he lost. Let's get real, their timing was kind of funny. Slow clap for Moderna chiming in the next week saying their vaccine was 95% effective. I don't know why people are still waiting for the vaccine if it was announced back in November. Which is why I say that Operation Warp Speed was more like Operation Slow as Molasses.

One final difficulty I had while making this research was the homeless situation in Los Angeles. 7-Eleven convenience stores are the unofficial transient meetup zone, and I did a lot of pickups from 7-Eleven—28 (5.5%) of the orders I did for this research were from 7-Eleven. Many customers ordered snacks and liquor from them late at night. Every park, every convenience store, every highway overpass have become *de facto* homeless shelters, and the politicians have been mostly ineffective in solving the problem. I know there's been progress with tiny homes being rolled out. The tiny homes are wonderful news, but the tiny home lots are still less than one hundred units at a time. I passed one hundred transients just on the last few blocks on the way to work today. What are the other fifty-eight thousand unhoused people in LA County supposed to do? The entire situation gives me a complicated feeling of pity, frustration, and anger, because it's sad for these people, and the very high taxes we pay in California are allegedly supposed to be alleviating this issue.

Having camps of homeless people in every park and corner changes the character of the neighborhoods, and every night I go to deliver it feels dangerous. I'm happy to give a couple dollars here and there. My heart is not made of icy obsidian. But when it's late at night and you have multiple people clearly blitzed out of their gourds on drugs loitering around the door of a 7-Eleven, it gets uncomfortable.

Out of the many, many unpleasant experiences I've had dodging crazed transients in Los Angeles, I leave you with the description of this one incident. I had stopped at a gas station in Marina del Rey to put air in one of my tires, since the "low air pressure" warning light that looks like an orange booty-hole had lit up.

I'm chilling in my car and examining images of Turkish muscle bears on Instagram after I fill my tire's air, and some dude with a patchy beard and yellow teeth scares me rapping on my window. Then he says, "You got a funny mouth. Do you suck dick for a living?"

I mean ... God willing. Where could I send my résumé? Was this an insult or an invitation? I had to pass on this occasion, but it made me think about my career options. If only I had the good business sense to charge for my affections when I was slightly younger, maybe I'd own a condo in Venice by now.

The Path to Dignity

My research provides a snapshot of eating habits in Los Angeles during this time of crisis. Basically, you'll have to view my study as about Beverly Hills in the way that *The Real Housewives of Beverly Hills* is about Beverly Hills. Sure, Lisa Vanderpump's Villa Rosa—a glamorous estate with a bunch of swans preening about a moat—is situated in Beverly Hills. But watchers of the series know that Erika Jayne lived 20 miles east in Pasadena, Dorit was over the hill in Encino, and Camille traded BH for Malibu. *Page 6* reports that Kyle Richards lives with her husband Mauricio in Encino, as well—it's not 90210 but when she's living in the Smokey Robinson Estate it's not exactly a downgrade. The long-winded ass point I'm trying to make is that Beverly Hills stands out in the American mind more as a metaphor for affluent living—a synecdoche for opulence deriving from the American media's content industry coming out of "Hollywood"—than it does for the measly 5.9 square miles the town occupies.

However, I did in fact learn a few interesting things about the legendary municipality. For example, 1995's *Clueless* gave an apt description of the geography when the character Josh teased the protagonist Cher, "You get upset if someone thinks you live below Sunset." North of Sunset Boulevard sits "The Hills"—a place where you have homes that fit into the "estate" or "manor" category—think the Greystone Mansion which you know from movies such as *Death Becomes Her* and *The Big Lebowski*. Not that Beverly Hills below Sunset is ramshackle or something—far from it—it's just not the same level of ostentatious.

Also, Beverly Hills surprised me in its diversity. In fact, every time a customer I delivered to in Beverly Hills came out to meet me for their delivery, it was either a black or Asian person. Which either means 1. Beverly Hills is more diverse than our current media portrays or 2. The white people who live in Beverly Hills don't come to their doors for deliveries. About half the time the app contained instructions for contact-free delivery where I just drop off the food, take a picture, and bounce, so I wouldn't know every customer's ethnicity, but Beverly Hills was more diverse than I had anticipated.

In addition to being fancy, chic, and fabulous, Beverly Hills struck me as slightly stuffy. However, the city still offers a taste of the Old Hollywood glamour that possesses a certain mystique. I completed 506 deliveries for my research, and I'm still driving now. Honestly, I sort of avoid Beverly Hills now that I'm done doing research, because I detest driving up the precipitous streets of The Hills at night. The streets are extremely narrow, you're on a cliff, and it's dark. I keep driving, because it's fun. I learn about different neighborhoods and get acquainted with new types of food.

I think for myself and for others, delivery apps will be remembered as a path to dignity during the pandemic era. The ease in doing gig work helped twofold: it allowed those in the most danger from the coronavirus to continue to be fed, and it helped those who required a financial stopgap to keep their dignity.

The *Correct* Names of Places in the Greater Los Angeles Area

One thing that's a challenge when people move to Los Angeles is they might feel overwhelmed by the sheer number of new place names they need to learn. I've been here just three years, but it has taken me this long to get used to some of the confusing places. For example, Huntington Park is nowhere near Huntington Beach. San Pedro is a street going through Skid Row, but it's also the name of a lovely oceanside community on the opposite side of Los Angeles. Santa Monica can refer to a city, an extremely long boulevard, or a mountain range. A bus going "to Venice" might actually be taking you away from Venice Beach to DTLA, because that bus is heading to its terminus along Venice Boulevard downtown.

Nowhere is the geography challenge more visible than the local weather forecasts, where women who look like bombshells tell you it's gonna be sunny and dry for the 100th day in a row. Many days I'll look at the forecasts and see these women prancing about in bandage dresses and think, "Is she about to go to the Golden Globes or tell me about this high pressure system?"

Anyway, without fail these forecasts will mention a neighborhood or community I've never heard of, and I'm always feeling lost. Thus, I make a series of ridiculous mnemonic devices for remembering them that I usually think up when bored while I'm driving. Here for your enjoyment are the *correct* names for places in the Greater Los Angeles area.

These names are not a commentary on the people living there. If I write "Rancho Cucaracha" for "Rancho Cucamonga," I don't actually think they have cockroaches. I'm just making jokes.

Apple Valley – Crapple Valley

Cahuenga Boulevard – Cawanker Boulevard

Centinela Avenue – Salmonella Avenue

City of Commerce – City of Commies

Diamond Bar – Diamond Barf

El Segundo – Smell Segundo

Granville Avenue - Brandi Glanville Avenue

Hawaiian Gardens – Hawaiian Garbage

Jardine Street – Sardine Street

La Tijera Boulevard – La Tiara Boulevard

Long Beach – Schlong Beach

Pasadena – Passa Deez Nuts

Simi Valley – Slimy Valley

Sylmar – Slimer

San Bernadino – San Berdoo

Whittier – Shittier

Ayres Avenue – Nothing is wrong with this street's name. Best street in Los Angeles. It's even spelled correctly.

Notes on Data Collection

The data I used comes from 506 deliveries made on Postmates, DoorDash, and Uber Eats in the months of September 2020 through December 2020. All deliveries were performed in Los Angeles county with about 90% of the deliveries being performed in Beverly Hills, West Hollywood, and nearby communities of western Los Angeles such as the neighborhood of Westwood and Santa Monica city.

The destination could be difficult to predict, and the deliveries took me as far west as the ocean (Venice/Manhattan Beach), as far north as Sylmar in the San Fernando Valley, as far East as Pico Rivera near East LA, and as far south as Long Beach.

For this research I had a policy of inclusion in that I tried to accept every order. I had intended to exclude all fast food orders, since I thought reading about fast food would be less interesting for my readers. I eventually decided against this method of research, since at some point it becomes difficult to distinguish between fast food and more artisanal restaurants. For example, it's clear that McDonald's or Taco Bell are fast food establishments, but what about Fatburger? Or Habit Burger Grill? Would Jersey Mike's fit into fast food like Subway clearly did, or did it fit into a category that implied higher quality?

To avoid this question—in which the answer can be quite subjective—I decided to accept all orders that I was pinged for throughout the duration of the case study. I only declined orders in which I felt accepting would put me in danger. For example, there were times I was too physically tired to drive the twisting roads of the Hollywood Hills at night. Or I would decline if I could see the destination would take me to an area known for violent crime. Sometimes I would I have two apps on, and they would both ping me at the same time, at which point I would accept the one that offered a higher payout because #getmoneybitch!

Having a policy of accepting every order—or turning on Uber Eats "auto-accept" function—does affect the statistics in that I would receive orders other drivers were avoiding because the payout was too low or the destination was in a less desirable neighborhood. Hence, I might start off the night in Beverly Hills, but Uber Eats would auto-accept each order sucking me further down into some dicey neighborhoods, at which point I would turn off auto-accept and drive back to ole Beverly.

Disclaimers Yadda, Yadda, Yadda

These statistics are approximate. I'm not liable for shit. Does the woman on the cover look like Marie Curie? Am I Nicolai Tesla? No, this is Charles St. Anthony, and you just read *Beverly Hills Postmate*. If I inspire you to Postmate and you sprain your ankle or somehow suffer economic hardship, guess what? Tough titty, 'cause it ain't my problem. It is not the problem of Charles St. Anthony, I.G. Studios LLC, my mom, my cousin, my housekeeper, or my dog. So I guess you'll just have to deal.

Don't mean to brag, but I usually got an "A" (but sometimes a "B") in algebra, which totally prepared me to whip up a spreadsheet in Google Sheets—I don't pay for Microsoft Office like a chump. Then, I use the filter function to find the answer to such pressing questions as how much McDonald's people ate or which type of Taco Bell sauce packet was the most popular.

I made every reasonable effort to bestow upon you, my glorious reader, with current and accurate information. I.G. Studios LLC makes no guarantee about the content, accuracy, or timeliness of this data. However, I had time to double-check my research, since we have been stuck in our houses for the last year. Use of the information and advice contained herein is entirely voluntary and at your sole risk (dun dun dun).

I.G. Studios LLC is not affiliated with any third party entities linked to or referred here. I don't get anything special from the restaurants. I work as an independent contractor for Instacart, Postmates, Uber, and DoorDash, but I am otherwise unaffiliated with these companies. They don't endorse me or anything like that (at least not yet).

If you found this book educational or entertaining, please consider purchasing my other books *Impossibly Glamorous*, *San Francisco Daddy*, *Uber Diva*, and *DTLA Hustler*—available as eBook, audiobook, and in print! Make sure to leave an online review of *Beverly Hills Postmate* on your favorite online retailer.

My diagnostics report suggests that by driving electric I avoided emitting 1,734 lbs. (787 kg) of CO_2 while driving 17,067 miles (27,467 km) in the last year.

Thank you for reading! Find me on social media! Drive electric!

Charles St. Anthony

Get Your Life

Stay in the know by signing up to my mailing list on my website dtlahustler.com. Support the content of Charles St. Anthony by becoming one of my Patreons at https://www.patreon.com/twithcharles.

Find me on social media on Instagram @kingcharles0921 or on Twitter @kingcharles0921.

First and foremost thank you to Marcella Hammer for your editorial input. I love you! Follow Marcella @marhammertime.

A heartfelt thanks to Anyadi Izuchukwu for her editorial assistance.

Thank you to Charles Ford who hand made my stylish and comfortable masks which you can get at https://ford-hand-made.square.site/.

I need to include a special thank you to TL Mason for your technical wizardry. Find him at https://www.fiverr.com/tlmason.

Thank you to my friends and family. Also, thank you to all the first-responders and medical professionals that risked their lives daily as our country grappled with the pandemic. Not only them, but also hugs and eternal gratitude to all our essential workers in supermarkets, restaurants, policemen, firemen, mass transit, and anyone else who helped keep our society running during 2020.

They are the true heroes.

For each of my books, I make a Spotify playlist as a "soundtrack." Listen to the soundtrack to *Beverly Hills Postmate* on Spotify.

Black Lives Matter. Please donate and support.

About Charles St. Anthony

Charles acquired his BA from Columbia University in East Asian Studies with an emphasis on Japanese language and culture. He went on to receive his MA in the same subject from Sophia University in Tokyo, Japan. He subsequently appeared on Japanese TV as a foreign commentator and personality on shows such as *Waratte ii Tomo!* (It's OK to Laugh) and *Goji ni Muchu!* (Infatuated at 5PM) where he was credited as Charles Ayres.

He has written for various publications and released several humorous memoirs including *Impossibly Glamorous* and *San Francisco Daddy*. His comedic short reads on the gig economy include this work, *Uber Diva*, and *DTLA Hustler*. He also hosts the podcast *T with Charles* in which he introduces notable personalities and takes a close-up look at the scalding hot topics of our time.

Establishments Mentioned

Avra Beverly Hills (https://theavragroup.com/avrabeverlyhills/)
233 North Beverly Drive – Beverly Hills, CA

California Pita (https://www.californiapita.com/)
242 South Beverly Drive – Beverly Hills, CA

Chocolate Bash (https://chocolatebash.com/)
10897 West Pico Boulevard – Los Angeles, CA

Crustacean Beverly Hills by House of An (https://crustaceanbh.com/)
468 North Bedford Drive – Beverly Hills, CA

El Paladar Oaxaqueño (http://elpaladaroaxaqueno.com/)
11654 Santa Monica Boulevard – Los Angeles, CA

Fat Sal's Deli (https://fatsalsdeli.com/)
972 Gayley Avenue – Los Angeles, CA

Honeybee Burger (https://honeybeeburger.com/)
The Colony at 11419 Santa Monica – Los Angeles, CA

Jersey Mike's (https://www.jerseymikes.com/)
279 South Beverly Drive – Beverly Hills, CA

Mama Hong's Vietnamese Kitchen (https://www.mamahongs.com/)
11819 Wilshire Boulevard – Los Angeles, CA

Shin-Sen-Gumi (https://shinsengumigroup.com/)
1601 Sawtelle Blvd. – Los Angeles, CA

Sprinkles Cupcakes (https://sprinkles.com/)
9635 South Santa Monica Boulevard – Beverly Hills, CA

Trejos Tacos (https://www.trejostacos.com/)
1556 Cahuenga Blvd. – Los Angeles, CA

Wally's (https://www.wallywine.com/)
447 North Canon Drive – Beverly Hills, CA

The Win~Dow at American Beauty
(https://www.americanbeauty.la/)
425 Rose Avenue – Venice, CA

References

Benjamin, Kathy. "How 5 Super-Rich Places Got Such Fancy Names." *Mental Floss*. March 20, 2012. Retrieved January 24, 2021.

The Bluebulb Project. The Measure of Things. Retrieved February 6, 2021.

Bochner, Braden and Juliette Deutsch. "Why Is There No Fast Food in This City." B*everly Highlights*. 2013, November 8. Retrieved December 30, 2020.

Clare, Nancie. "How Fame Came to Beverly Hills." *The Hollywood Reporter*. 2014, March 29. Retrieved January 24, 2021.

Clare, Nancie. "How the World's First Movie Stars Made Sure Beverly Hills Didn't Become Part of LA." *LAmag.com*. 2018, February 20. Retrieved December 30, 2020.

Clueless. Heckerling, Amy (director). Rudd, Paul (performer). 1995. Film.

CPI Inflation Calculator. Inflation Calculator. Retrieved February 6, 2021.

"History of Beverly Hills." Municipal Website of the City of Beverly Hills. *Beverlyhills.org*. Retrieved January 24, 2021.

Hopkins, Pamela. *The History of Beverley, East Yorkshire.* Blackthorn Press: 2003.

Inflation Calculator (website). Retrieved January 2021.

Madell, Lisa Johnson. "Kyle Richards buys lavish 'Smokey Robinson Estate' for $8.3M." *Page Six.* 2017, October 30. Retrieved January 30, 2021.

Richard, Olivia, et al. "First Tiny Home Community Opens in LA, with 75 Beds for Unhoused Angelenos." *LAist.* 2021, February 4. Retrieved February 11, 2021.

Stalh, Max. "Who Is Beverly, Anyway?" *Beverly Highlights.* 2014, January 24. Retrieved December 30, 2020.

Sumagaysay, Levi. "The pandemic has more than doubled food-delivery apps' business. Now what?" *MarketWatch.* Edited for clarity. 20, November 25. Retrieved January 28, 2021.

Swanson, Ana. "Why So Many of America's Sushi Restaurants Are Owned by Chinese Immigrants." *The Washington Post.* 29, September 2016. Retrieved February 14, 2021.

Wanamaker, Marc. *Early Beverly Hills.* Arcadia Publishing: 2005.

Fin.